JAMES MADISON

The Presidents of the United States

George Washington
1789–1797

John Adams
1797–1801

Thomas Jefferson
1801–1809

James Madison
1809–1817

James Monroe
1817–1825

John Quincy Adams
1825–1829

Andrew Jackson
1829–1837

Martin Van Buren
1837–1841

William Henry Harrison
1841

John Tyler
1841–1845

James Polk
1845–1849

Zachary Taylor
1849–1850

Millard Fillmore
1850–1853

Franklin Pierce
1853–1857

James Buchanan
1857–1861

Abraham Lincoln
1861–1865

Andrew Johnson
1865–1869

Ulysses S. Grant
1869–1877

Rutherford B. Hayes
1877–1881

James Garfield
1881

Chester Arthur
1881–1885

Grover Cleveland
1885–1889

Benjamin Harrison
1889–1893

Grover Cleveland
1893–1897

William McKinley
1897–1901

Theodore Roosevelt
1901–1909

William H. Taft
1909–1913

Woodrow Wilson
1913–1921

Warren Harding
1921–1923

Calvin Coolidge
1923–1929

Herbert Hoover
1929–1933

Franklin D. Roosevelt
1933–1945

Harry Truman
1945–1953

Dwight Eisenhower
1953–1961

John F. Kennedy
1961–1963

Lyndon Johnson
1963–1969

Richard Nixon
1969–1974

Gerald Ford
1974–1977

Jimmy Carter
1977–1981

Ronald Reagan
1981–1989

George H. W. Bush
1989–1993

William J. Clinton
1993–2001

George W. Bush
2001–present

JAMES MADISON

DAN ELISH

mc **Marshall Cavendish**
Benchmark
New York

11/07

Marshall Cavendish Benchmark
99 White Plains Road
Tarrytown, NY 10591-9001
www.marshallcavendish.us

All Internet addresses were correct and accurate at the time of printing.

Library of Congress Cataloging-in-Publication Data

Elish, Dan.
James Madison / by Dan Elish.
p. cm. — (Presidents and their times)
Summary: "This series provides comprehensive information on the presidents of the United States
and places each within his historical and cultural context. It also explores the formative events of his
times and how he responds"—Provided by publisher.
Includes bibliographical references and index.
ISBN 978-0-7614-2432-1
1. Madison, James, 1751–1836—Juvenile literature. 2. Presidents—United States—Biography—
Juvenile literature. I. Title. II. Series.
E342.E44 2007
973.5'1092—dc22
[B]

Editor: Christine Florie
Publisher: Michelle Bisson
Art Director: Anahid Hamparian
Series Designer: Alex Ferrari

Photo research by Connie Gardner

Cover photo by The Granger Collection

The photographs in this book are used by permission and courtesy of: *The Granger Collection:* 3, 6,
8, 10, 17, 19, 22, 28, 36, 39, 42, 47, 49, 51, 52, 56, 60, 63, 65, 82, 85, 86(R), 86(L).
Corbis: Bettmann, 16, 25, 33, 42, 44, 58, 61, 71, 73, 74, 76. *Art Resource:* Reunion des Musees
Nationaux, 26, 87 (L). *Getty Images:* Hulton Archive, 83, 87 (R).

Printed in Malaysia
1 3 5 6 4 2

CONTENTS

James Madison, sometimes referred to as the father of the Constitution, was one of the nation's most influential founding fathers.

A POLITICIAN GROWS UP

James Madison, America's fourth president, is possibly the country's most overlooked founding father. Benjamin Franklin was a great wit, political thinker, and inventor. Thomas Jefferson drafted the Declaration of Independence. George Washington served as a general of the Continental army and was the country's first president. At first glance, James Madison does not measure up to these giants of American history. He certainly did not look the part of a confident leader of a boisterous new nation. He stood only 5 feet 4 inches tall, and his friends sometimes said that he was "never bigger than half a bar of soap." Madison was so pale and thin that the famous American author Washington Irving went so far as to call him "withered."

A quiet man, Madison wore dark clothes and was usually content to let his outgoing wife, Dolley, do the talking at parties. Even in Congress he spoke softly. But even though Madison could not deliver a speech with the force of his fellow Virginian Patrick Henry, the power of his ideas almost always made him the most respected man in the room. Madison's contributions to the forming of his country may not have been as colorful as those of other founding fathers, but they were equally, if not more, important. After America won the Revolution against Britain, the young country still had to set up a workable government. Despite his serving two terms as president, in which he led the nation through the War of 1812 (sometimes called America's second revolution),

Madison is best known for what he did earlier as a principal architect of both the U.S. Constitution and the Bill of Rights.

"Never have I seen so much mind in so little matter," one observer said. It is not an exaggeration to say that without James Madison, the U.S. government as we know it today may never have existed.

BOYHOOD

James Madison was born on March 16, 1751, in Virginia, then still a colony of England. Known as "Jemmy" to his family,

Young James Madison was raised by a prosperous Virginia family and received an excellent education.

Madison was the oldest of twelve children. His father, also named James, owned a large tobacco and wheat plantation called Montpelier. Like most women in colonial America, his mother, Eleanor Rose "Nellie" Conway Madison, spent most of her waking hours tending the garden and making clothes, candles, and soap, as well as raising the children.

Young James was a small boy with blue eyes and a sensitive face. Though often in poor health, he played with his brothers and sisters as well as the children of his father's many slaves. But Jemmy was first and foremost a bookworm. Instead of riding and hunting, he often preferred to spend time in his father's library. Taught how to read and write mostly by his grandmother, he had devoured all eighty-five books in the house by age eleven. After his grandmother died, Madison's father enrolled him in a boarding school 70 miles away that was run by a Scots-

Madison attended the College of New Jersey in 1769, graduating two years later, in 1771.

man named Donald Robertson. There, Madison studied Greek, Latin, French, philosophy, and math with the sons of other well-off children. Later, Madison would say of Robertson, "All I have been in life I owe largely to that man."

At sixteen Madison left Robertson's school, in 1767, when his father called him home to study with a new tutor, the Reverend Thomas Martin. In Madison's day the college of choice for wealthy Virginians was the College of William and Mary in Williamsburg, Virginia. When it was time to start, though, Madison was ill. His family worried that the low ground of Williamsburg would prove unhealthy for him. Worse, students at William and Mary had a reputation for drinking and playing cards. With the encouragement of his tutor, Madison decided instead to attend the College of New Jersey (now Princeton University).

At the time young Jemmy had never been out of Virginia. But if he was worried about making the 300-mile journey, there is no record of it. Traveling by horseback, he set out with two friends and a slave. Today, the drive from Virginia to Princeton takes only five or six hours. In Madison's time it took almost ten days. Negotiating dangerous ferry crossings on the Rappahannock, Potomac, and Susquehanna rivers, Madison made his way to Princeton, New Jersey, excited to start a new chapter in his life.

TROUBLE WITH BRITAIN

At college young James became caught up in the political events of his day. At the time of Madison's birth, most Americans were perfectly happy to live under the rule of the British crown. That began to change after the French and Indian War (1754–1763),

Bostonians protest the Stamp Act by burning stamps in a bonfire.

in which British troops won control of Canada. When the war was over, King George III of England decided that the American colonies should pay their fair share for its costs. Thus, in 1765 he imposed the Stamp Act, a law that forced American colonists to pay taxes on newspapers, legal documents—even playing cards. Many colonists were furious. Not allowed seats in the English Parliament—after all, the English government met in London, across the Atlantic Ocean—the colonists complained of "taxation without representation." In October 1765 a patriot named Samuel Adams arranged for the colonies to send representatives to New York to come up with a response to the British tax. This so-called Stamp Act Congress passed a resolution that called for the American colonies to **boycott** British goods. Six months later, faced with colonial discontent, King George III backed down. In 1766 the taxes of the Stamp Act were stopped.

But more taxes were to come. Over time colonial anger at the British and the monarch grew. In college Madison became a pupil of Princeton president John Witherspoon, a forty-seven-year-old Scotsman the students called "Old Doctor." "Just by

COLLEGE LIFE

College students in James Madison's era certainly worked hard—they had to! A student's time was regimented from dawn to dusk. At Princeton the wake-up bell rang at 5:00 A.M. An hour later there was a bell for morning prayers. After that Madison and other students would study for an hour before breakfast, then report to classes, which ran until one in the afternoon. After lunch, classes reconvened at three o'clock and ran until five. Then came the bell for evening prayers. Worst of all, someone checked to make sure that all students were in their rooms either studying or sleeping by nine o'clock.

With these kinds of rules, it is no wonder that Madison achieved in college. But he also found time for some fun. A practical joke of the day involved greasing chicken feathers, leaving them on pathways, and watching people slip. Other pranks were ringing the chapel bell at night, lighting firecrackers in a new student's room, and spying on girls through telescopes.

reason of being what they are," Witherspoon asserted, "people have certain God-given rights. These rights are not and cannot be given by kings and taken away by kings." Like many young colonists, Madison found such words inspiring. Soon he was taking time from his studies to participate in protests against the British. When more taxes were levied on the American colonies, Madison and his fellow students supported new boycotts of British goods. When the colony of New York sent a message to the merchants of Philadelphia suggesting that they break the boycott, Madison and his fellow students intercepted the letter and gleefully threw it on a bonfire. On graduation day, as a protest, all the seniors wore clothes made of homespun American cloth, as opposed to more finely made English broadcloth.

Madison graduated from Princeton in thirty short months. But he had worked so hard at his studies, he was too weak to attend his own graduation. Not feeling up to the long trip home, Madison stayed on in Princeton and studied Hebrew and theology with the Old Doctor. But in April 1772 his father insisted that he return to Virginia to help tutor his brother William and his sisters.

By the time he got back to Montpelier, Madison was utterly exhausted. He suffered from what he called "sudden attacks, somewhat resembling epilepsy." On top of that, he was bored. After two and a half exciting years away at school, life on the farm seemed dull. Madison split his time between tutoring his younger brother and sisters and studying law, which he found "dry and coarse."

Then came horrible news. A college friend, Joe Ross, had died. Despondent, Madison wrote another Princeton friend, William Bradford, in Philadelphia, "I am too dull and infirm now to look out for any extraordinary things in this world for I think my sensations for many months past have intimated to me not to expect a long or healthy life." Properly concerned, Madison's parents sent him to Warm Springs, West Virginia, a spa where the mineral waters were supposed to cure a range of illnesses. Madison drank the water by the gallon, but his health did not improve. Back home a doctor looked at his skinny frame and suggested that he go horseback riding for exercise. That didn't help much, either.

In the end what healed young James Madison was his interest in his country. As the colonies and England edged closer to war, Madison found a passion in politics that lifted his spirits and led him to his life's work: government.

FREEDOM OF RELIGION

When war broke out with England, James Madison and all other young men of his social standing were expected to lead a regiment. In 1775 he was **commissioned** as a colonel of the Orange County militia. Unfortunately, on the first day with his troops, Madison fainted. Undeterred, he threw himself into the role of soldier and was soon bragging to his friends about his expert aim with a rifle. Even so, his military career was short-lived. Madison's fellow citizens recognized that he was more of a thinker than a fighter. In 1776 he was elected to represent Orange County at the Virginia Constitutional Convention, convened to create a new state government free of British control. It was there that Madison made his first small contribution to American politics.

At Princeton, Dr. Witherspoon had believed strongly in a person's right to worship as he or she pleased. From that idea Madison had become a vigorous proponent of freedom of religion. When the established church of Virginia imprisoned Baptist preachers in 1773, Madison had been outraged. That same year he wrote to William Bradford in Philadelphia:

I have neither patience to hear talk or think of any thing relative to this matter, for I have squabbled and scolded, abused and ridiculed so long about it, to so little purpose that I am without common patience.

Madison asked Bradford to send him a copy of Pennsylvania's colonial charter so he could better understand "the extent of your religious toleration." After reading the document from his friend, Madison congratulated him for living in a state, Pennsylvania, where religious freedom was honored. Madison vowed that he would fight to ensure that his fellow Virginians had the same rights.

Madison was one of the youngest **delegates** at the Virginia Convention, and most certainly the smallest. In an effort to remain unnoticed, he dressed in black and often whispered his ideas to his fellow Virginian Edmund Randolph. But as he matured, Madison showed the ability to overcome his natural shyness and speak out on behalf of his firmly held principles. The first draft of the state's Declaration of Rights promised "that all men should enjoy the fullest toleration in the exercise of religion, according to the dictates of conscience." Though considered a **liberal** position for its day (at that time there were many countries that did not allow their citizens any religious freedom), Madison was not yet satisfied. Yes, the state would "tolerate" the free exercise of religion, but the language of the first draft still did not proclaim that the state could not, if it wanted, deny a citizen those rights. In Madison's view the right to freedom of religion was born within each individual. Accordingly, he persuaded the convention to change the wording to say that "all men are equally entitled to the free exercise of religion, according to the dictates of conscience." In Madison's version the state did not have the right to deny a citizen his right to worship as he chose. Late in his life Madison wrote:

> *I have no doubt that every new example will succeed, as every past one has done, in showing that religion and Government will both exist in greater purity the less they are mixed together.*

THE FIRST CONTINENTAL CONGRESS

After his successful debut at the Virginia Convention, Madison was eager to make politics his career. His timing could not have been better. In 1775, with the battles of Lexington and Concord (April 19) and Bunker Hill (June 17) in Massachusetts, the Revolutionary War had begun. On July 4, 1776, the Continental Congress adopted the Declaration of Independence, in which the colonies asserted their independence from Great Britain, listing many grievances against the king. In 1777 Madison ran for a seat in the Virginia House of Delegates. But his success in working on the Declaration of Rights made him overconfident. Madison knew that he was smarter and better prepared than most men, but he did not know much about how to win an election. At that time it was customary for a candidate to win supporters by providing free drinks, but Madison objected to "the corrupting influence of spirituous liquors." Refusing to supply alcohol to the voters, Madison lost.

Though deeply hurt by that defeat, Madison was elected the same year to serve on the Council of State, which advised Virginia's governor. Two years later he was one of four delegates chosen to represent Virginia at the Continental Congress in Philadelphia. At that point the United States was in a state of crisis. Two years

The drafting committee of the Declaration of Independence presents its work to John Hancock, the president of the Continental Congress.

earlier, in 1777, the Continental Congress had created a document called the Articles of Confederation, a sort of pre-Constitution, that spelled out how the new American government would work. When Madison arrived in Philadelphia, these articles had not been passed into law by all the states because of a dispute regarding western land rights.

Even so, several years before the articles were finally passed in 1781, it was already obvious to Madison that they were far too weak. Tired of living under a powerful king, most Americans were afraid that a strong central government would be just as bad. As a result the Articles of Confederation defined the country as no more than "a firm league of friendship" among the thirteen states. There was a Congress that made laws, but it couldn't make the states pay taxes or raise an army. There were no courts to enforce the laws. There wasn't even a president. Each state considered itself an **independent** nation with the power to make whatever laws it wanted.

The result was that the government was not able to raise taxes to support an army. Money was short. Inflation was rising. Madison's rent for staying at a boardinghouse for the first three months of his stay in Philadelphia was a whopping $20,000! In his first report to the Virginia governor at that time, Thomas Jefferson, Madison described the state of the country:

Drafted in 1777 by the Continental Congress, the Articles of Confederation established a "firm league of friendship" among the thirteen states.

> *Our army threatened with an immediate alternative of disbanding. . . . ; the public treasury empty; public credit exhausted, . . . Congress complaining of the extortion of the people; the people [complaining] of the improvidence of Congress, and the army of both. . . . These are the outlines of the true picture of our public situation.*

Madison served three frustrating years as Virginia's delegate in Philadelphia. Time and again he proposed ways to give the federal government more power over the states. Time and again he was defeated. Still, though the wife of Virginian Theodorick

YOUNG LOVE

Quiet. Shy. Tiny. Brilliant. These are all adjectives used to describe James Madison. No one would have ever called him dashing or romantic. Until he finally married at age forty-three, Madison had had only one short-lived romance.

In 1783, while serving in the Continental Congress, Madison lived in a boardinghouse. There he met Kitty Floyd, a beautiful fifteen-year-old who was visiting Philadelphia with her parents and sisters. In Madison's era a teenage girl was considered ready for marriage. At thirty-two Madison looked much younger, and Kitty's father encouraged the young girl to spend time with Madison, by then a well-respected congressman. Soon the couple announced their engagement. When plans were made for a November wedding, Thomas Jefferson wrote his friend, "I rejoice at the information that Miss K. and yourself concur in sentiments."

Unfortunately, Miss K. was really in love with a nineteen-year-old student. In July, while in New York, Kitty sent Madison a short letter breaking off the engagement. Madison was crushed. In letters to Jefferson he complained of Kitty's "indifference." Though Madison eventually went on to a happy and long marriage, he carried the bitterness toward Kitty Floyd throughout his life. Fifty years later, while going through his papers, he inked out all references to her name.

Bland called Madison "a gloomy, stiff creature," his fellow congressmen quickly came to appreciate his sharp mind. At the end of his term Madison served on the Virginia legislature. There he tried to persuade the people of his home state to give up some of their power for the sake of a stronger central government. Again he failed.

SHAYS'S REBELLION

Then came an event that forced American leaders to take a harder look at the failings of their government. During the summer of 1786 Daniel Shays, a Massachusetts farmer and Revolutionary War veteran, led seven hundred farmers and workers to protest unfair taxes and the loss of their voting rights. The uprising lasted on and off until the winter of 1787, when the State of Massachusetts was forced to hire **mercenaries** to stop it. Though Shays escaped to Vermont, two other instigators of the revolt were hanged. Many Americans, including George Washington, were alarmed at the state of affairs. Washington wrote to Madison,

Government troops and Shays's rebels encounter one another at the arsenal in Springfield, Massachusetts.

Without some alteration in our political creed, the superstructure we have been seven years raising at the expense of much blood and treasure, must fall. We are fast verging to **anarchy** *& confusion!*

The famous revolutionary John Adams also wondered whether a collection of states could function together as a union. "The lawgivers of antiquity . . . legislated for single cities," he noted, but "who can legislate for 20 or 30 states, each of which is greater than Greece or Rome at those times?"

Madison was determined to meet the challenge. Together with the New Yorker Alexander Hamilton, he called for a meeting in Annapolis, Maryland, to discuss trade and other issues among the states. Unfortunately, delegates from only five states attended. Undeterred, Madison and Hamilton called for another meeting. This one would be in Philadelphia and would address a broader topic: how to rewrite the Articles of Confederation.

THE CONSTITUTIONAL CONVENTION

Two

*J*ames Madison was determined to fix America's system of government. But before he could start, he had to convince the **delegates** from other states in the Union to attend the convention that he and Alexander Hamilton had arranged. Despite the government's obvious flaws, many Americans, fearful of creating a central government with too much power, remained wary of tampering with the Articles of Confederation. To counteract his countrymen's suspicions, Madison knew that the gathering needed a leader who had the unqualified respect of the nation—a man who would give it automatic legitimacy. In young America there was only one person who fit the description: George Washington.

Unfortunately, Washington was busy enjoying his retirement after the Revolutionary War. The last thing he wanted to do was leave his farm in Virginia to travel all the way to Philadelphia to oversee a group of men haggling over small points of law. Moreover, Washington was a hero, known worldwide for leading the American Revolution. If the Constitutional Convention failed, he knew that his reputation would be tarnished. Nevertheless, Washington was as eager as anyone to see the United States attain the strong footing of a well-run government.

From the beginning, Madison negotiated with the great general very carefully. When Washington refused Madison's first request that he attend the convention, Madison asked the governor of Virginia, Edmund Randolph, to appoint Washington as the

George Washington presided over the Constitutional Convention in 1787.

leader of the Virginia delegation. Madison then begged Washington not to reject the offer—at least not immediately—knowing that Washington's name would signal to other states that the upcoming convention was a gathering they could not miss. In the end Washington not only attended but served as the convention's president.

Preparations for the convention took many months. As winter turned to spring, the country began to sense that something very important was afoot. One newspaper stated, "The political existence of the United States perhaps depends on the result of the Convention which is to be held in Philadelphia in May next."

JEMMY PREPARES

In 1787 the Continental Congress usually met in New York City. But at that time Philadelphia was the capital city in spirit, boasting, according to the historians Christopher Collier and James Lincoln Collier, "excellent libraries, eight newspapers, [and] several magazines." Philadelphia had a bustling population of 45,000 people, and the streets were paved in brick or stone, unusually splendid for the time. Homes were commonly two stories high. Philadelphia also had 117 taverns, or small inns, where people boarded, ate, drank, and socialized. It was in the taverns of Philadelphia that most of the fifty-five delegates to the convention stayed.

Though the convention was slated to begin on May 14, James Madison arrived eleven days early and took up lodging in a boardinghouse run by Mrs. Mary House. One of Madison's greatest strengths was his meticulous preparation. All that winter and spring he had been studying other systems of government. He researched confederacies throughout history, showing how their lack of a strong central authority caused their failure. Madison wrote some of his ideas in letters to Thomas Jefferson, who was currently serving as America's ambassador to

A bustling Philadelphia in front of Independence Hall during the late 1700s.

France. He also remained in close contact with George Washington. On April 16, 1787, he wrote the commander:

I would propose next that in addition to the present federal powers, the national Government should be armed with positive and complete authority in all cases which require uniformity; such as the regulation of trade, including the right of taxing both exports & imports.

MADISON'S "VICES"

In preparing for the Constitutional Convention, James Madison drafted a list that he called "Vices of the Political System of the United States":

1. Failure of the States to comply with the Constitutional requisitions.
2. Encroachments by the States on the federal authority.
3. Violations of the law of nations and of treaties.
4. Trespasses of the States on the rights of each other.
5. Want of concert in matters where common interest requires it.
6. Want of Guaranty to the States of their Constitutions & laws against internal violence.
7. Want of sanction to the laws, and of coercion in the Government of the Confederacy.
8. Want of ratification by the people of the articles of Confederation.
9. Multiplicity of laws in the several States.
10. Mutability of the laws of the States.
11. Injustice of the laws of States.
12. Impotence of the laws of the States.

Madison used his days in Philadelphia for more than private study. Realizing that he would have a better chance of getting the type of government he wanted if he had the support of other delegates, Madison met with his fellow Virginians each morning after breakfast, going through his ideas point by point. It was not long before Madison convinced his colleagues of the inadequacy of the Articles of Confederation. By the time the convention started its work, the Virginia delegation had agreed to speak with one voice.

THE GREAT COMPROMISE

By May 25 enough delegates had arrived in Philadelphia for the convention to convene. Every state except Rhode Island had sent delegates. As expected, George Washington was elected president of the convention. At age eighty-one Benjamin Franklin was

Benjamin Franklin was the oldest delegate at the Constitutional Convention.

James Madison
said of the creation
of the Constitution,
"[The Constitution
of the United
States] was not,
like fable Goddess
of Wisdom, the off-
spring of a single
brain. It ought to
be regarded as the
work of many
heads and many
hands."

the oldest delegate. At age twenty-seven Jonathan Dayton of New Jersey was the youngest. About half had gone to college, and half were lawyers. Some came from small states, others from big ones. Some were from the South, others from the North. Seventeen of the delegates together owned over 1,400 slaves.

Thomas Jefferson (who was still in Paris) called the delegates "demi-Gods." The historian James MacGregor Burns described them more humorously as "the well-bred, the well-fed, the well-read, and the well-wed." By any measure they were a talented and well-educated group of men, eager to give their country's government a desperately needed jump start. Of all of them, Madison was perhaps the most impressive. As William Pierce of Georgia wrote, "Every person seems to acknowledge his greatness."

Great, perhaps—but Madison was smart enough to appreciate his weaknesses. Despite his brilliance, he was not a powerful

DOUBLE DUTY

During the Constitutional Convention, James Madison sat by George Washington's side, recording events of the day in his own system of shorthand, then transcribing them out more fully at night. Participating in the stressful meetings by day and writing out the transcripts by night was brutal work. Madison later wrote that it "almost killed" him. But it's lucky for students of American history that Madison made the effort. The only surviving record of the convention, his transcription of the Constitutional Convention, is a priceless American artifact.

James Madison lacked public speaking skills and depended on his fellow delegate and governor of Virginia Edmund Randolph to speak for him at the convention.

and charismatic speaker. For that reason he asked his old friend, the handsome and well-spoken Edmund Randolph, fellow delegate and governor of Virginia, to present his ideas to the convention. Randolph agreed. On May 29 he rose to his feet and laid out the main points of what historians call the Virginia Plan.

The Articles of Confederation were flawed in many ways. Perhaps the stricture that needed to be amended most urgently had to do with how many votes each state would receive in the new Congress. In 1787 Massachusetts, Virginia, and Pennsylvania had almost half of the country's population. Accordingly, they thought the number of representatives in Congress should be based on how many people lived in each state. The smaller states had a different idea. Their delegates came to Philadelphia already worried that the big states would grab too much power. They felt that each state should have an equal number of votes, no matter how tiny its population.

Madison hailed from a well-populated state, and his Virginia Plan called for a legislature, or Congress, with two houses, both based on proportional representation. The lower house would be elected by the people. It would, in turn, elect members of an upper house. In Madison's plan the Congress would hold the most power, more than the president, setting foreign policy and appointing a national treasurer. Needless to say, the small states did not like Madison's proposed government at all. George Read of Delaware threatened that should Madison's system of representation be approved, "it might become their [the Delaware delegation's] duty to retire from the Convention."

By June discussions were boiling over into shouting matches. Soft-voiced Madison rose to speak over two hundred times that summer. But all the careful reasoning in the world could not persuade all the delegates to accept his plan. Eventually William Paterson proposed the New Jersey Plan, in which each state should have one vote in Congress. Madison was distressed. To him it seemed obvious that each state should have votes in

PRIVACY IN PHILADELPHIA

When the Constitutional Convention began, James Madison and the other delegates made a striking security decision. Even though the temperature in Philadelphia was in the nineties, the windows would stay shut. Moreover, guards would be placed in the halls, and delegates would not be allowed to write letters to their loved ones at home about what was happening.

Why the secrecy?

The delegates knew that every citizen in the country had a strong opinion about how the nation should be run. No matter what kind of government was formed, some Americans would be angry. If word of the discussions leaked too soon, some delegates feared that riots could erupt.

Congress in proportion with its population. On June 19 Madison addressed the convention, saying, "The great difficulty lies in the affair of Representation; and if this could be adjusted, all others would be surmountable." But that was easier said than done. As the hot summer reached late June, things looked so bad that Benjamin Franklin suggested they start each session with a prayer. George Washington looked so downcast that some delegates said he had "that Valley Forge face."

YOU ARE THERE

Imagine yourself a delegate at the Constitutional Convention. The question before you is whom to count for determining the number of congressmen from each state. Of the people who are not slaves, should you count women (remember, they cannot vote), children, aliens, and free African Americans?

If all the slaves are counted, estimates are that the slave states would be very close to having a majority in the House of Representatives, which would be unacceptable to northern delegates. But if none of the slaves are counted, estimates are that the slave states would have about 40 percent of the representatives, unacceptably low to southern delegates. There are mutterings of walking out of the convention in that case. There is a proposal to count three-fifths of the slaves as a compromise, which would give the slave states about 47 percent of the seats in the House, which both sides would begrudgingly accept.

How would you vote?

It looked as though the convention was going to fall apart. Then Roger Sherman, the delegate from Connecticut, suggested that Congress be divided into two separate parts, or houses—the House of Representatives and the Senate. In the House of Representatives the well-populated states would get more votes than the states with smaller populations. In the Senate each state would have the same number of votes. Sherman actually made the same proposal a month before and had been shouted down. But a month of arguing had made the delegates ready to work together. Sherman's plan was called the Great Compromise.

The Convention Takes on Slavery

At the time of the Constitutional Convention, Madison said, "The great danger to our general government is the great southern and northern interests of the continent being opposed to each other." Indeed, America's first eighty years under the Constitution were marked by great discord over the issue of slavery—discord that exploded in 1861 into the Civil War. But in 1787 the issue with slaves was not so much whether they should be freed but whether they should count for representation in Congress.

Not surprisingly, southern states wanted their slaves counted as full citizens—that way those states would get more votes and thus more power. But the northern states thought that was ridiculous. If the South considered their slaves as property, why should the slaves be counted as people? It seemed that the delegates would never agree. Finally, another compromise was suggested, this time by James Wilson of Pennsylvania. He proposed that when people were counted to figure out how many representatives each state would have, the total number of

Madison and Slavery

Like many of the other southern delegates to the Constitutional Convention, James Madison was a slaveholder. As a boy Madison played with the children of his father's slaves. He took a slave with him on his first trip to Philadelphia, on his way to college. As an adult his views on what was known as the "peculiar institution" of slavery were extremely conflicted. Deep down, Madison felt slavery was wrong. On the other hand, he did not see how the economy of the South, which included his family's plantation at Montpelier, could function without slave labor. Madison also could not envision how whites and blacks might possibly live together. Like many men of his era—even men who were considered enlightened—he felt that the only rational solution to the problem was the establishment of a black settlement in Africa for American slaves. At the same time, slavery would be abolished. He wrote:

> [It] might prove a great encouragement to manumission [freeing slaves] in the Southern parts of the U.S. and even afford the best hope yet presented of putting an end to the slavery in which not less than 600,000 unhappy negroes are now involved.

The nation of Liberia (now the Republic of Liberia) on the west coast of Africa was actually founded by African Americans, but did not prove to be the hoped for promised land.

During the Constitutional Convention delegates discussed whether to count slaves as full citizens or to consider them property without voting rights.

slaves in a state would be divided by three-fifths. The idea of counting a human being as only a little more than half a person seems shocking today. Madison and many of the other delegates did not like it much either, but they accepted it. Wilson's compromise saved the day, and the meetings in Philadelphia kept going.

CHECKS AND BALANCES

Soon it was early September of 1787. Delegates had come and gone all summer. Over six hundred deals had been struck. But all their hard work had paid off. James Madison and the other fifty-four delegates had created a government that was made up of three branches: executive, legislative, and judiciary. The executive branch, or the president, was to serve a four-year term. The legislative branch, or the Congress, would be made up of the House of Representatives and the Senate and would make the laws. The judiciary branch, or the courts, would interpret the laws.

Following Madison's concept, the delegates made sure that their new government had checks and balances. In other words, for every power the delegates gave to one branch of the government, they gave another branch a way to counteract that power.

James Madison was quick to give others credit for their work in formulating the constitution. But despite the secrecy of the proceedings, in the days after the convention word of his stunning contribution spread. Madison was the best-prepared and most knowledgeable delegate. Though an uninspiring **orator**, his logical, well-thought-out positions usually carried the day. Again, William Pierce of Georgia described his abilities best:

> *Mr. Madison is a character who has long been in public life. . . . He blends together the profound politician, with the scholar. In the management of every great question he evidently took the lead in the Convention, and though he cannot be called an Orator, he is a most agreeable, eloquent, and convincing Speaker.*

*T*hough Madison emerged as a hero of the Constitutional Convention, it did not mean that all of the American people were lining up to shake his hand. Perhaps the delegates were right to keep their discussions secret. When the new constitution was finally made public, many people were shocked. After all, under the Articles of Confederation the federal government had almost no power. And now? Now there were two houses of Congress and a president. Indeed, with the constitution down on paper, the delegates' work was really just beginning: they had to get the people to accept it. Worse, they already knew that Rhode Island, which had not even sent a delegation to the convention, would say no. That was why Madison and the other delegates made the decision that if two-thirds, or at least nine, of the state conventions voted yes, the constitution would become the law of the land.

The country quickly split into two camps. Some Americans called themselves **Federalists**. That group favored a strong central government and supported the new constitution. They were opposed by the Anti-Federalists, who thought that the new constitution took too much power away from the states. As tempers rose, an Anti-Federalist newspaper went so far as to call Benjamin Franklin "a fool from age" and George Washington "a fool from nature."

The Federalist Papers

Clearly, Americans needed some convincing. At the end of the convention many of Madison's friends urged him to hurry back to

Virginia to start defending the constitution to his state **caucus** immediately. Instead, Madison chose to travel to New York, where the Continental Congress was in session. It was a good decision. Worried that the New York ratifying convention was going to turn down the new constitution, Alexander Hamilton and fellow New Yorker John Jay had begun writing a series of essays later published and called *The Federalist Papers* that defended the constitution. Hamilton's first essay claimed that the

THE

FEDERALIST:

ADDRESSED TO THE

PEOPLE OF THE STATE OF NEW-YORK.

NUMBER I.

Introduction.

AFTER an unequivocal experience of the inefficacy of the subsisting federal government, you are called upon to deliberate on a new constitution for the United States of America. The subject speaks its own importance; comprehending in its consequences, nothing less than the existence of the UNION, the safety and welfare of the parts of which it is composed, the fate of an empire, in many respects, the most interesting in the world. It has been frequently remarked, that it seems to have been reserved to the people of this country, by their conduct and example, to decide the important question, whether societies of men are really capable or not, of establishing good government from reflection and choice, or whether they are forever destined to depend, for their political constitutions, on accident and force. If there be any truth in the remark, the crisis, at which we are arrived,

The Federalist Papers, *a series of eighty-five essays written for New York voters, argued that the proposed constitution was what was right for the country.*

series would "endeavor to give a satisfactory answer to all the objections [about the constitution] which shall have made their appearance, that may seem to have any claim to your attention."

At the time Madison was exhausted from the convention. Still, he agreed to help with the writing. In the end eighty-five essays were written. Because of illness, Jay put down his pen after writing only five. Of the remaining essays Hamilton is said to have written fifty-two and Madison twenty-eight. Published

THE FEDERALIST PAPERS

Madison's first essay in the *Federalist* is considered one of the most brilliant pieces of writing in American history. In the following passage he discusses the challenges that face any government in making sure that minority rights are not forgotten in the face of an "overbearing majority."

Complaints are everywhere heard from our most considerate and virtuous citizens, equally the friends of public and private faith, and of public and personal liberty, that our governments are too unstable, that the public good is disregarded in the conflicts of rival parties, and that measures are too often decided, not according to the rules of justice and the rights of the minor party, but by the superior force or an interested and overbearing majority. However anxiously we may wish that these complaints had no foundation, the evidence of known facts will not permit us to deny that they are in some degree true.

In "Federalist No. 51" Madison famously wrote, "If men were angels, no government would be necessary."

from October 1787 through August 1788 under the name "Publius," the Federalist essays appeared initially in three New York newspapers: the *Independent Journal*, the *New-York Packet,* and the *Daily Advertiser*. Jefferson called them "the best commentary on the principles of government as ever was written." More important, after their initial publication in New York, Hamilton made sure that the essays were circulated to other states with strong anti-constitution sentiment. Many historians agree that *The Federalist Papers* helped convince many skeptical Americans that the new constitution was well worth approving.

Bringing the Case to Virginia

In late 1787 the states began to vote. The small states of Delaware, New Jersey, and Georgia **ratified** the constitution quickly. Pennsylvania also voted yes and, by a narrow margin, Massachusetts also voted in favor. Despite the success of *The Federalist Papers*, the vote looked to be extremely close in New York and Virginia.

Again James Madison rose to the occasion. Although suffering from stomach problems, he rushed home to Montpelier. In order to speak to the Virginia delegation, he first had to win a seat as a delegate. With the election slated for the day after he arrived, Madison put himself up as a candidate. The shy man who hated to speak in public even gave a campaign speech, or as he called it, "a harangue of some length in the open air and on a very windy day." When the votes were counted, Madison had won by a slim margin. With the Virginia ratification convention set for June, Madison got busy arguing the case for the new constitution. He had a formidable adversary, Patrick Henry, an ardent supporter of states' rights, a brilliant orator, and one of the most popular men in Virginia.

Patrick Henry addresses the Virginia Assembly, arguing against the constitution.

When the date for debate arrived, the State House proved too small to seat all 170 delegates. Instead, the men met in a nearby concert hall. Patrick Henry spoke first, declaring that the constitution would create "one great consolidated empire." He warned that the president would be no more than a king.

Henry spoke for hours. He did not stop even when he was interrupted and told that his wife had given birth. But eventually it was time for the Federalists to defend their work. As he had done at the Constitutional Convention, Madison let the more eloquent Edmund Randolph speak first. But on June 6, 1788, the third day of debate, Madison took the floor. As usual, he swayed the crowd with quiet but logical argument:

We ought . . . to examine the Constitution on its own merits solely: we are to inquire whether it will promote the public happiness: its aptitude to produce this desirable object ought to be the exclusive subject of our present researches. In this pursuit, we ought not to address our arguments to the feelings and passions, but to those understandings and judgments which were selected by the people of this country, to decide this great question by a calm and rational investigation.

Speaking in a voice so soft that those in the back had to strain to hear, Madison went through the constitution point by point. He pointed out its checks and balances: how the president needed Congress's permission to declare war; how the Senate and House of Representatives could override a presidential veto. How could this system be called an empire? The debate raged. Madison grew ill and had to miss four days, leaving others to argue his case. When he returned on June 11, Madison took the floor again and spoke persuasively. On June 21 New Hampshire became the ninth state to vote in favor of the constitution. Even so, colonial citizens knew that the constitution would be effectively worthless without the support of two of the country's biggest states, Virginia and New York. On June 25 the Virginia delegation finally voted. The constitution was approved by a vote of 89 to 79. A month later New York also signed on. The U.S. Constitution was the law of the land.

New York celebrates with a parade following the ratification of the Constitution on July 26, 1788.

THE BILL OF RIGHTS

Now that the country had a new Constitution, it was time to elect a government. From the last months of 1788 through the beginning of 1789, each state held its own election. On April 6 the votes were finally counted. To no one's surprise, George Washington was elected the country's first president.

Madison was eager to continue his career in politics—so eager, in fact, that directly after the Virginia delegation voted to approve the Constitution, he went back to New York to resume his duties in Congress. When George Washington tried to persuade him to run for the Senate created under the new Constitution, Madison said he preferred to serve in the House of Representatives. But winning the election was not so easy. His old rival Patrick Henry drew up the state congressional districts so that Madison's primary base of support would be diluted. Henry then asked James Monroe, later America's fifth president, to run against Madison. In order to win the election, Madison was forced to make a promise. Some Americans were upset that the Constitution did not include a statement of the basic human rights that would be guaranteed to every citizen. Madison pointed out that most states had so-called bills of rights in their own constitutions and that the new Constitution guaranteed Americans their basic rights already. The issue had also been discussed in *The Federalist Papers*. In "Federalist No. 84" Hamilton worried that a bill of rights would have the opposite effect than intended. If a list of rights were written down, Hamilton argued, later generations might interpret it as a list of the *only*

George Washington takes the oath of president at New York's City Hall.

rights that people had. He went on to write that "the Constitution is itself, in every rational sense, and to every useful purpose, A BILL OF RIGHTS."

Thomas Jefferson saw the issue differently. Writing from France, he told Madison that "A bill of rights is what the people are entitled to against every government on earth."

In the end Madison realized that more Americans would support their new government if a bill of rights were part of the package. Once elected to the House of Representatives, he promised to introduce the appropriate amendments. He wrote that

amendments, if pursued with a proper moderation and in a proper mode, will be not only safe but may serve the double purpose of satisfying the minds of well meaning opponents, and of providing additional guards in favour of liberty.

After Washington was sworn in as president, Madison got to work. On June 8, 1789, he made a speech in Congress proposing a list of amendments to the Constitution to protect the political and legal rights of individuals. It took two and a half years, but on December 15, 1791, ten amendments were passed by both houses of Congress and ratified by three-quarters of the state legislatures and became known as America's Bill of Rights. They guaranteed Americans everything from the right to a speedy trial to the right to bear arms. Perhaps most important of all to Madison was the First Amendment, which guaranteed freedom of speech and religion—and of the press. As he put it later in his career, "[T]he right of freely examining public characters and measures, and of free communication among the people thereon . . . has ever been justly deemed the only effectual guardian of every other right."

THE PARTNERSHIP WITH JEFFERSON

Four

At the beginning of George Washington's eight years as president, James Madison was one of his most loyal and trusted advisers. From Madison's time overseeing the Constitutional Convention, Washington knew perhaps better than anyone how thoroughly Madison understood the Constitution. Time and again in the early days of his presidency, Washington called on Madison to interpret the new laws of the land. In a real way Madison deserves some of the credit for one of Washington's greatest characteristics: as president he was very careful to obey the law and not overstep the bounds of his constitutionally granted powers. Indeed, Washington respected Madison so much that he had him draft his first inaugural address. As a member of the House of Representatives, Madison then wrote the congressional response to the president about the same speech. To top it off, Madison then drafted Washington's thank-you letter back to Congress!

James Madison and Thomas Jefferson strongly believed that the power of the states should hold sway over the federal government.

Unfortunately, by the end of Washington's presidency the

warm relationship between the two men had soured. The reasons had more to do with changes in the outlook of Madison than of Washington. To be sure, from the days of the Articles of Confederation, Madison had been a strong proponent of a powerful central government. But once Washington came into power, Madison found himself siding with Secretary of State Thomas Jefferson—a man who believed that the bulk of the power in the United States belonged with the individual states. Together, Jefferson and Madison became the leaders of a new political party called the Jeffersonian-Republicans or sometimes the Democratic-Republicans. John Quincy Adams, America's sixth president, described their partnership as "a phenomenon, like the invisible and mysterious movements of the magnet in the physical world." For his part Washington remained aligned with his secretary of the treasury, Alexander Hamilton, a man who firmly believed in a strong central government. Together, Washington and Hamilton became the leaders of the Federalist Party.

COMPROMISE IN 1790

When George Washington took the oath of office as the first president of the United States, the country was in a serious financial hole. Years of revolution and scant tax collection had left the fledgling U.S. treasury bankrupt. In 1790 the debt of the United States was $77.1 million, an enormous amount in those days. Both Madison and Hamilton wanted America to clear its debts. But Madison began to differ with the Washington administration in his ideas of how Hamilton should go about it. Hamilton wanted the national government to take responsibility for the debts piled up from the war. He suggested that to pay them off, the federal government should sell bonds. Madison objected, arguing that some states, including Virginia, had already paid off their war debts. Why should the national government have to go into debt to pick up the financial slack for **fiscally** irresponsible states? Hamilton's proposal did these states an injustice, Madison said, by "compelling them, after having done their duty, to contribute to those states who have not equally done their duty."

Other aspects of Hamilton's financial fix for the country bothered Madison as well. During the Revolutionary War the government had been short of money. As a result soldiers had been paid with certificates that they could redeem for hard currency when the government was solvent. But many poorer soldiers, desperate for money, had sold their certificates to speculators at a low price. Was it fair that these speculators now be allowed to cash in the certificates at full value while the soldiers who had fought bravely in the war got nothing? Madison and many other Americans were furious over the situation. "Never have I heard more rage expressed against the Oppressors of our Country during the late War," said Benjamin Rush, a well-known revolutionary, "than I daily hear against the men who . . . are to reap all the benefits of the revolution, at the expense of the greatest part of the Virtue and property that purchased it."

At the same time there was heated discussion about the location of America's capital. Northerners favored keeping it in New York or Philadelphia. But Madison, Jefferson, and many southerners wanted it to be in the South. Eventually, a compromise was reached. Madison and Jefferson supported Hamilton's economic plan, and a new city, Washington, District of Columbia, was created on the borders of Maryland and Virginia for the nation's capital.

In 1791 Maryland and Virginia ceded land that would become the nation's capital of Washington, D.C.

Yet, despite this one compromise, Madison and Jefferson continued to grow more and more distressed by the Washington administration. Hamilton favored the establishment of a national bank. Madison thought it was unconstitutional and would favor the business elite over the poor. Washington approved it. In 1793 Washington signed the Proclamation of Neutrality in which America backed out of the 1778 Treaty of Alliance with France, wherein the United States and France had agreed to fight on each other's behalf. Realizing that the young nation wasn't ready for war, Washington asserted that America would not take sides in a war between Britain and France. Madison was outraged and even accepted an honorary French citizenship, an honor that Washington and Hamilton both turned down.

The National Gazette

Madison and Jefferson were so frustrated with Washington's policies that they undertook to oppose them by any means possible. In May of 1791 they traveled the North trying to recruit like-minded citizens to join the cause. In New York the two men asked one of Madison's college friends, Philip Freneau, to start a newspaper in Philadelphia that would stand in opposition to Washington's policies. Freneau eventually founded the *National Gazette*. Madison contributed a series of anonymous articles to it, all critical of the Washington administration. Over time, however, Freneau's attacks on Washington grew so vicious that Jefferson and Madison were embarrassed by them. Worse, they could not do anything to stop him without having to admit that they were the ones who encouraged him to start the paper in the first place. As at the Constitutional Convention, secrecy was paramount. When Madison once misplaced an article he had written for the paper, he anxiously wrote Jefferson, "The possibility of its falling into base hands cannot be too carefully guarded against. I beg you to let me know its fate the moment it is in your power."

Marriage—At Last

While engaged in bitter feuds with George Washington and Alexander Hamilton, James Madison at long last fell in love. In 1793 an epidemic of yellow fever swept through Philadelphia, claiming four thousand lives. Among the dead was John Todd Jr., a lawyer. His widow was Dolley Payne Todd, a blue-eyed, pale-skinned woman who was said to be such a beauty that men would station themselves near her home in hopes of catching a peek as she walked by. In the spring of 1794 Madison asked a college friend, Aaron Burr, later vice president of the United States, to arrange an introduction. Dolley was flattered, writing a friend that "the great little Madison has asked . . . to see me this evening."

The two could not have been more different. Though one of the leading lights of the nation, Madison, now forty-three years old, remained a small, shy man who always dressed in black. Dolley was twenty-six, bubbly, funny, well dressed, and fashionable. Despite a seventeen-year age difference, their first meeting was a success. Dolley was able to bring out the quiet humor and kindness in Madison's personality. Within a few months James proposed to vivacious Dolley.

The delightful Dolley Payne Todd married James Madison in September of 1794.

But even though Dolley respected Madison enormously, she was not sure if she was ready to get married again so quickly, especially to an older man. Needing time to think it over, she visited her sister, leaving Madison in Philadelphia to await her answer. "[Mr. Madison] thinks so much of you in the day," a friend wrote Dolley, "that he has Lost his Tongue, at Night he Dreams of you." In August Dolley finally made up her mind. The answer was yes. Even so, on her wedding day a month later, she still harbored doubts. Before the ceremony, she wrote a friend, "In this union I have everything that is soothing and grateful in prospect—and my little Payne [her son] will have a generous and kind protector." She signed using her maiden name, "Dolley Payne Todd." But later that night, after the wedding, she added a postscript to the note that suggested her misgivings. "Evening—Dolley Madison. Alass! Alass!"

Happily for Madison, his bride's doubts soon disappeared. By all reports Dolley's admiration for her older husband soon turned to genuine love, although there were to be no children. A decade after their marriage she wrote Madison, "A few hours only have passed since you left me, my beloved, and I find nothing can relieve the oppression of my mind by speaking to you in this the only way." Later she added, "Our hearts understand each other."

FOREIGN AFFAIRS

Given the ongoing frustrations of his political career, James Madison must have been grateful for his happy marriage. In 1792 George Washington had been reelected as president and continued to support policies at home and overseas with which Madison intensely disagreed.

In 1789 the French people had revolted. King Louis XVI was **deposed** in 1791. At first most Americans were pleased that the French were claiming their independence. But it soon became clear that the French Revolution was bringing chaos to France's streets instead of reform. Moderates were killed, and the new leaders began a reign of terror. Then, in 1793 Britain and France

Citizens of Paris storm the Bastille, the city's largest prison, obtaining arms at the outbreak of the French Revolution in 1789.

went to war, and Americans began choosing sides. In general, Jefferson, Madison, and the people of the South and West remained loyal to the French, who had helped them fight and win their own war of independence. But George Washington, Hamilton, and most northeasterners favored Britain.

At the beginning of Washington's administration the United States enjoyed trade with many countries across the Atlantic. But as hostilities overseas continued, French and British ships began to stop and board American merchant ships on the way to Europe. Worse, the British navy impressed American sailors, forcing them to join the British navy. While it was true that some

Captured American soldiers were forced to leave their ships and board British vessels and join Britain's navy.

of these American sailors were in fact British deserters, most of the men forced to sail for Britain were actually citizens of the new United States. England did not care, citing the theory of "perpetual allegiance," which claimed that any sailor born under British rule continued his allegiance to the mother country, even if he had lived in the United States since boyhood. Needless to say, Americans were outraged at this treatment. On top of seizing hundreds of American ships, British troops in Canada (which they controlled) were supporting Native-American tribes that persisted in harassing settlers in the Ohio Territory. During Washington's second term it appeared more and more likely that the two countries would once again go to war.

In 1794 Washington dispatched James Monroe to France and John Jay to England to try to devise a way to keep the peace. Jay returned home first with a treaty called, appropriately enough, the Jay Treaty. In it the British agreed to vacate their western forts by June of 1796 and to compensate American ship owners for seized vessels. In return America gave Britain "most favored nation" status and agreed to pay pre-Revolutionary War debts. The treaty also firmed up boundaries in the Northeast. But more important to the Jeffersonians was what the treaty did not do. Britain refused to allow trade between America and the West Indies, which was very profitable for America. More crucially, it did not address the issue of British impressment of American seamen.

By the time the treaty was signed, Thomas Jefferson had already given up on trying to influence George Washington and had resigned from his Cabinet. That left Madison to spearhead the good fight from the House of Representatives. Unfortunately, Madison's attempt to discredit the treaty turned into one of the lowest moments in his public life. As a principal architect of the Constitution, Madison had made clear in the Constitutional Convention and in *The Federalist Papers* his belief that the Senate was the house of Congress with the authority to approve foreign treaties. Even so, the minute the Senate approved the Jay Treaty, Madison backed a House initiative calling on Washington to produce a record of how the treaty was negotiated, hoping to discover evidence of some sort of corruption that would allow the House of Representatives to overrule the Senate. Furious, Washington turned over a copy of the minutes of the Constitutional Convention to the State Department. The notes showed that Madison had agreed that the House of Representatives could not affect the Senate's ability to make treaties. So in the end Washington had the final say. The vote in the House of Representatives on the treaty went against Madison. From that time forward the great general and Madison rarely talked. When Washington retired to Virginia after his terms in office, he did not invite Madison to visit him at his Mount Vernon estate.

Madison's years in the House of Representatives were frustrating. Time and again his ideas and policies were defeated by Washington and Hamilton, his old friends. Worse, when George Washington's two terms were finished, John Adams, another Federalist, was elected as the country's second president. Having had enough of politics, Madison decided to retire. In 1797 he returned with Dolley to Montpelier to look after his farm. But politics was in Madison's blood. In a very short while he found himself getting drawn back into the political issues of the day.

The Road to the Presidency

*J*ames Madison did his best to enjoy his retirement. He read good books, wrote long letters, and oversaw construction on his house. When a delegation of Democratic-Republicans asked him to run for the Virginia state legislature in 1799, he said no. Only when Madison found out that his opponent would be his old rival Patrick Henry did he change his mind. He was easily elected.

But even as he went back to work in Richmond, the Virginia state capital, Madison was becoming increasingly alarmed by events in Washington, D.C., and Europe. Like George Washington, President John Adams found himself spending his four years in office trying to avoid a conflict with either Britain or France. It was not easy. After the signing of the Jay Treaty, a furious France began seizing American ships. Moreover, French rulers refused to receive America's newly appointed ambassador. When Adams sent three more envoys to France, they were secretly approached by three go-betweens, later referred to as X, Y, and Z, who demanded a hefty bribe from the Americans for the privilege of talking with Charles Maurice de Talleyrand, the French foreign minister. Just like that, Americans were as angry at the French as they had been at the British!

It was in this climate that Adams signed off on a set of laws that drew James Madison back into national politics. With many Federalists clamoring for war against France, the Federalist majority in Congress passed the Alien and Sedition Acts in 1798,

On May 20, 1798, in response to President John Adams's (above) Alien and Sedition Acts, James Madison wrote to Thomas Jefferson that the "Alien bill proposed in the Senate is a monster that must forever disgrace its parents."

a set of laws that they insisted were needed to protect American national security from agents of the French.

In truth, these laws denied Americans basic rights, giving the president the authority to deport any alien he found threatening and making it illegal to publish "false, scandalous, and malicious writing" against the government. Jeffersonians were properly outraged. After all, the laws stood in direct opposition to the liberties Americans were supposed to enjoy.

In the colonial era the runner-up in a presidential election became the vice president. In 1796 that was Thomas Jefferson, loser in the election to John Adams. Jefferson was so upset by the Alien and Sedition Acts that he withdrew from his rightful post as president of the Senate and returned to Virginia, though he was still vice president. There he recruited Madison to help him find a way to overturn the hated laws.

The Virginia and Kentucky Resolutions

To fight John Adams and the Federalist Congress, Jefferson and Madison decided to write a series of resolutions that called for the nullification of the despised Alien and Sedition Acts. But as the sitting vice president, Jefferson could not very well be on record as fighting against his own administration. As a result he and Madison decided to submit their resolutions anonymously to the state legislatures of Kentucky and Virginia. Their basic argument was that since the federal government had exceeded its constitutional powers in regard to the Alien and Sedition Acts, "nullification" was the only "rightful remedy."

In 1798 Jefferson wrote the Kentucky Resolution, claiming that the Alien laws violated the First Amendment, which promised all Americans freedom of speech. "[U]nless arrested at the threshold," Jefferson wrote, these laws will "necessarily drive these states into revolution and blood." In 1798 the Virginia legislature approved a similar, if less inflammatory, resolution written by Madison that called on other states to agree that "the acts aforesaid are unconstitutional; and that the necessary and proper measures will be taken by each, for co-operating with this state."

Jefferson and Madison hoped that their resolutions would start a groundswell of resistance to the Alien and Sedition Acts. In the end, however, no other state joined in. Indeed, just as the Federalists overstepped the bounds of the Constitution when they passed the Alien and Sedition Acts, Jefferson and Madison overstepped it in their reaction. Yes, the Alien and Sedition Acts violated the First Amendment, which promised freedom of speech to all Americans. But the attempt by Jefferson and Madison to overrule the government by claiming that individual states had the right to nullify federal laws was equally unconstitutional. In the end the Alien and Sedition Acts were allowed to expire in 1801.

SECRETARY OF STATE

In 1800 Thomas Jefferson was elected president. One of his first acts was to ask James Madison to serve as his secretary of state.

MARBURY V. MADISON

Today, if Congress passes a bad law, the Supreme Court can rule that it is unconstitutional. When the Federalist Congress passed the Alien and Sedition Acts, however, the Supreme Court was not the powerful body it is today. In the early years of America's history most of the appointed justices did not take the job seriously. On the day of the court's first session only three of the six justices even bothered to show up.

In 1801, before leaving office, John Adams appointed his secretary of state, John Marshall (below), to be the court's chief justice. It did not take Marshall long to assert new and dramatic power for the Supreme Court. In 1803, in a case called *Marbury v. Madison* (William Marbury was suing Secretary of State James Madison about a federal appointment), Marshall introduced the country to the concept of judicial review, or the right of the court to review the laws passed by Congress and, if necessary, to declare them unconstitutional and therefore null and void. As Marshall wrote in his opinion, "[A]n act of the legislature, to the constitution, is void." In one bold stroke Marshall made it clear that the Supreme Court had the enormous power to strike down federal laws and thus shape the workings of the government.

Madison quickly accepted. Unfortunately, he was unable to attend his friend's inauguration on March 4, 1801. In the last week of February his father had died. After taking care of his father's estate and recuperating from a brief illness, Madison was finally ready to set out from Montpelier to Washington. His trip was difficult. The roads of the era were terrible, and heavy spring rain turned them into a series of mud holes. Still, Madison and Dolley arrived at the newly founded nation's capital pleased that the Democratic-Republicans were in power at last. Jefferson had referred to his election as president as "a bloodless revolution." The Madison scholar Robert Allen Rutland explains:

When Madison and Jefferson spoke of the Boston "Monocrats" they believed beyond all doubt that moneyed men in the shadow of Beacon Hill really wished to see America living under a monarch who would found on American shores an imitation of the British royal family.

Accordingly, Jefferson and Madison set out to undo Federalist policy, cutting taxes and reducing the size of the army and navy.

As secretary of state Madison soon found himself grappling with the same basic problem that had plagued both Washington and Adams: how to keep the country out of war with either Britain or France. On the high seas English and French navies continued to harass American ships. In the West American pioneers were controversially setting up homesteads near English forts. Worse, British soldiers were said to be arming Native Americans.

To Jefferson and Madison's dismay, Napoleon Bonaparte, the militant ruler of France, was threatening war on neighboring

In April 1803 James Monroe, along with French ministers, agreed to the U.S. purchase of the French-held Louisiana Territory for $15 million.

countries. Worse, France controlled the Louisiana Territory, a gigantic tract of wild land to America's west. Worried that Napoleon might use the territory to invade the United States, Jefferson and Madison sent James Monroe to France to see if America could buy the city of New Orleans to ensure America's shipping rights on the Mississippi River. Fortunately, by that time Napoleon was focused on the activity of the British. Uninterested in America, he sold the United States the entire Louisiana Territory for only $15 million. Overnight, the territory controlled by the United States was increased by 828,000 square miles!

The Embargo

In 1804 Thomas Jefferson was elected to a second term in the White House. As secretary of state Madison's problems continued. War continued to rage in Europe, and the British navy was determined not to allow neutral nations to trade with France. On June 22, 1807, a British warship named the *Leopard* stopped an American frigate called the *Chesapeake*, and the captain demanded that the American captain turn over four sailors the

DOLLEY IN WASHINGTON

When the Madisons moved back to the nation's capital in 1801, Dolley Madison quickly made their home the center of Washington social life. Discarding the more conservative ways of her Quaker upbringing, Dolley, while very respectable, showed a liking for shopping, beautiful dresses, feathered turbans, and snuff (tobacco). An observer of the day remarked, "She looked a Queen. . . . It would be *absolutely impossible* for any one to behave with more perfect propriety than she did."

With Thomas Jefferson a widower, the president often asked Dolley to receive ladies at the White House and to serve as presidential hostess. On top of that, she bought furniture for Jefferson's home and dresses for his two married daughters. Later, when her own husband was elected president, Dolley presided over the first inaugural ball in 1809 and became known for her ability to smooth over quarrels. When the British burned the White House to the ground during the War of 1812, she calmly saved important records, as well as a famous painting of George Washington, before escaping in a carriage.

Englishman claimed were British deserters. When the captain of the *Chesapeake* refused, the *Leopard* opened fire. In the end three men were killed, eighteen were wounded, and the British impressed the four American sailors.

Americans were outraged, especially when King George III ordered the British navy to continue to impress American sailors. Desperate to avoid a war with England, Madison came up with a plan he hoped would keep the peace. On December 22, 1807, Congress passed the Embargo Act, a law that called for an immediate halt to all American shipping to Europe. Madison hoped that by depriving European countries of needed American goods, Britain and France would be forced to show the United States more respect on the seas. As Madison wrote:

> *The efficacy of an* **embargo** *. . . cannot be doubted. Indeed, if a commercial weapon can be properly crafted for the Executive hand, it is more and more apparent to me that it can force nations . . . to respect our rights.*

Madison's embargo lasted for the final fifteen months of Thomas Jefferson's presidency. Regrettably, instead of hurting Britain, the embargo hurt the United States. An economic depression gripped the country that crippled American businesses, especially in the Northeast. In 1808 American exports were barely a fifth of what they had been in 1807. To counteract the embargo's effects, smugglers ran goods from America, mainly across the Canadian border.

Despite overwhelming resistance and evidence of its failure, Madison stubbornly believed in his embargo to the bitter end, maintaining that if it were only enforced a bit better and allowed to last a short while longer, then it would work. In the declining months of Jefferson's presidency, Madison wrote to American diplomats that "the public mind everywhere is rallying to the policy." In truth, that simply wasn't true. Furious citizens rearranged

An American political cartoon satirizes Thomas Jefferson being robbed by King George III (left) and Napoleon Bonaparte (right) as a result of his embargo policy.

the letters in "embargo" to read "O Grab Me," "Go Bar 'Em," and "Mob Rage." One poet from New England expressed the views of many Americans by writing:

> *Our ships all in motion*
> *Once whiten'd the ocean;*
> *They sail'd and return'd with a Cargo;*
> *Now doom'd to decay*
> *They are fallen a prey*
> *To Jefferson, worms, and EMBARGO.*

Faced with torrents of public fury, Congress finally repealed the embargo, effective March 1, 1809, just three days before Jefferson's retirement. And even though James Madison had been the driving force behind one of Jefferson's most ineffective policies, by that time he had already been elected the fourth president of the United States.

When Thomas Jefferson announced that he would not be seeking a third term as president, James Madison, his right-hand man, became the obvious choice to succeed him. Despite the failures of his embargo policy, Madison himself remained popular. With the Democratic-Republican Party strong in the South and West, Madison easily defeated the Federalist Charles Pickering. On March 4, 1809, James Madison took the oath of office. Watching his old friend step into his shoes as commander in chief, Thomas Jefferson later wrote, "Never did a prisoner released from his chains feel such relief." Indeed, James Madison stepped into the White House in perilous times. English and French ships continued to harass American merchant ships and, in England's case, to forcibly impress American sailors. At war with each other, Britain and France imposed **blockades** on the other, making it even harder for American ships to reach

In his inaugural address Madison said "the present situation of the world is indeed without a parallel and that our own country full of difficulties."

European ports. Still, Madison was determined to find a way to keep the peace. Delivering his inaugural address, he asserted his hopes:

To cherish peace and friendly intercourse with all nations having correspondent dispositions; to maintain sincere neutrality towards belligerent nations; to prefer in all cases, amicable discussion and reasonable accommodation of differences, to a decision of them by an appeal to arms.

Unfortunately, James Madison was to find that remaining neutral in the face of war overseas was easier said than done.

THE MARCH TO WAR

President Madison still believed that his failed embargo could yet compel England and France to respect American rights at sea. So when Congress repealed it, he signed the Nonintercourse Act, which called for no trade with Britain and France for one year. Soon thereafter Madison received what seemed to be a lucky break. Early in his term the British foreign minister in America, David Erskine, informed him that England was planning to lift its Orders of Council, the set of laws that denied U.S. trading rights with other countries. Thrilled to be resuming trade, six hundred ships soon left American ports, sailing for England. But before the ships reached British shores, word came from England that Erskine was wrong. Britain would not be rescinding its Orders of Council. Normal trade would not be resumed. Britain would not give up its right to stop American ships and impress its sailors. To top it all off, Erskine was removed from his post.

Deeply disappointed, Madison scrambled for ways short of war to improve relations with Europe. When the Nonintercourse Act expired in 1810, Madison signed Macon's Bill No. 2, an act that stated that if either England or France dropped restrictions on American commerce, the United States would cease its nonintercourse restrictions on the other. In other words Madison attempted to bribe Britain or France into respecting America's rights. Napoleon Bonaparte took the bait, announcing that France would stop harassing American ships. In March of 1811 Madison responded by opening trade with France but not Britain. It was a fateful decision. England was furious that America had sided with its archenemy. To make matters worse, France continued to seize American ships anyway!

Against his wishes, Madison found himself impelled toward a declaration of war. He was pushed further by a wave of younger politicians from the South and West who were elected to Congress in 1810. Tired of hearing their fathers' war stories about victories over the British, this new breed of politicians craved their own battlefield glory. Those from the West were eager to fight Native Americans north of the Ohio River, many tribes that were armed by British troops. But more than anything, these "war hawks" saw a golden opportunity to win the United States new territory. With English troops pinned down fighting Napoleon in Europe, many Americans thought it would be simple to invade British-controlled Canada. In 1812 Thomas Jefferson said, "The acquisition of Canada this year . . . will be a mere matter of marching." Spurred by continued British seizures at sea and the clamoring of the war hawks at home, Madison finally made up his mind. On June 1, 1812, he asked Congress for a declaration of war against Britain. Most northeasterners, historically pro-British, objected. But a coalition of southerners and westerners gave Madison the votes he needed. Ironically, the day *before* the United States declared war, Britain agreed to repeal its Orders of Council. But in the days before cablegrams, telephones, or e-mail, news traveled very slowly. By the time word of the British action reached American shores, the war had begun.

WHY BRITAIN?

Why did the United States go to war with Britain and not France? For one thing, though Britain had seized 917 American ships since 1803, the French had taken only 558. And England was America's historical rival. In addition, Madison's Democratic-Republican Party was traditionally pro-French. Still, the overriding reason that the United States chose to fight England had to do with Canada. Henry Clay of Virginia swore that the country could be taken by his state's militia alone. It is true that America resented the British impressment of its sailors. But that would not have mattered if Canada had not seemed ripe for the plucking. As for Madison, he hoped that when deprived of needed Canadian goods, Britain would collapse.

John Randolph of Virginia described the tenor of the Congressional war debates:

Ever since the report of the Committee on Foreign Relations came into the House, we have heard but one word—like the whippoorwill, but one monotonous tone—Canada, Canada, Canada.

THE WAR PRESIDENT

Unquestionably, James Madison was a brilliant political thinker, a man who understood possibly better than any other in American history the inner workings of government. But his presidency demonstrated that the qualities it takes to write a constitution and to pass legislation in Congress are different from those required to be an effective commander in chief. Though Madison gradually rose to the challenge of being a wartime leader, the opening year of the conflict was marked by disaster.

Poor Leaders

From the start of his administration, James Madison hurt his ability to wage an effective war by choosing unqualified people for important Cabinet posts. The secretary of war was William Eustis, whose only military service was as a surgeon during the Revolution. The secretary of the navy, Paul Hamilton, was a former governor of South Carolina who was known to drink too much. Instead of moving Albert Gallatin, Jefferson's secretary of the treasury, to the position of secretary of state, where Jefferson wanted him, Madison appointed Robert Smith, a man he did not trust. Worst of all, Madison refused to fire an army general, James Wilkinson, who had failed to obey an order to move troops away from malarial swamps in New Orleans, thereby consigning many to death. The biographer Robert Rutland wrote of the "Wilkinson Affair,"

> [B]y dodging his responsibility, Madison harmed the war effort, hurt the army's morale, and in effect became a buck-passer instead of a courageous leader.

A Poorly Trained Army

As secretary of state Madison had favored a small army, a fact that came back to haunt him once the war began. Despite a population of a million men of age to fight, the United States managed to get only seven thousand together for any particular battle. The ill-trained regular army was supplemented by even more poorly trained state militias. Many of these "soldiers" ran away from battle. Perhaps most damaging of all, a number of American generals were relics of over age sixty from the Revolutionary War, men who had not led troops into battle for years. Some of the worst were weeded out as the war went on, though by that point American dreams of taking Canada had been lost.

Money Problems

James Madison knew better than anyone that wars take money. "War is the parent of armies," he wrote in 1795. "From these proceed debts and taxes." But during the War of 1812 he crippled the nation's ability to raise money to fund the fighting. While George Washington was president, Alexander Hamilton had put America's finances on a firmer footing. At Hamilton's urging, Congress had established the Bank of the United States. As it turned out, the bank's charter was due to expire in 1811, a year before the war began. Though Madison had called the bank unconstitutional when it was originally established, he was inclined to renew its charter anyway. Quite simply, his embargo had thrown the United States into an economic depression. Madison needed the bank to grant the loans that would fund the war. Secretary of the Treasury Albert Gallatin pleaded with Congress to renew the bank's charter. Unfortunately, the war hawks thought the bank favored the moneyed elite and fought against it—using Madison's old arguments!

Not wanting to be accused of switching positions, Madison stayed on the sidelines of the debate. The result was that Congress voted not to renew the bank. Consequently, the War of 1812 had to be fought using funds only from taxes, without bank loans. In 1815, with the war over, Madison finally addressed Congress, saying, "the benefits of an uniform national currency should be restored to the community." That same year the bank was rechartered.

The Canadian Strategy

The war itself began with high hopes. With Canada firmly in its sights, the United States attacked. But those who thought their northern neighbors would be ripe for the plucking had misjudged Canada's willingness to fight. Many Canadians were Loyalists to the British crown who had been driven north during the Revolution. Having no interest in becoming American citizens, they fought hard. Some historians feel that American troops might have had a chance if they had focused their meager army on an attack on Montreal. Instead, American troops attempted a three-pronged invasion. Brigadier General William Hull, an aging veteran of the Revolution, led

American general William Hull surrenders at Detroit during the War of 1812.

the first prong from the outpost of Detroit. Hoping to attack a British post at Fort Amherstburg, Hull's army crossed into Canada on July 12, 1812. After some skirmishes Hull decided he could not attack the fort without artillery and retreated. Two other attacks—one across the Niagara River and the other along Lake Champlain toward Montreal—were beaten back by the formidable Canadians. Just like that, Madison's grand war plans were in shambles.

The Navy and Reelection

When the United States finally began to win some battles, it was in a way no one had expected; it was with its navy. At the start of hostilities in 1812 the British navy was the undisputed king of the seas, sailing nearly eight hundred men-of-war. Of these, 191 were ships of the line (those that carried between sixty and eighty guns), and 260 were the smaller frigates. For its part the United States had no ships of the line and only seven frigates. Fortunately for Madison, the frigates America did have were extraordinary ships, built by the naval architect Joshua Humphreys during the Washington administration. Constructed of sturdier wood than the British ships, these vessels carried more men and guns. Ironically, while in Congress, Madison had opposed their construction, arguing that "to send ships of force among the armed powers would entangle us in the war if anything would do it."

Despite Madison's initial objections to their construction, it was one of Humphrey's frigates that gave the United States its first victory in the war. On August 19, 1812, the U.S. frigate *Constitution*, nicknamed "Old Ironsides," defeated the British frigate *Guerriere* off the coast of Newfoundland. Though this battle had no real impact on the war's outcome, it did wonders for American morale. It also helped Madison in his bid for reelection in 1812.

The USS Constitution *battles and overcomes the British* Guerriere.

With the North fervently against what they called "Mr. Madison's War," Madison was able to point to some sort of military success in his campaign against opponent DeWitt Clinton of New York. With many westerners itching for revenge after General Hull's defeat at Detroit, Madison eked out a victory. To his credit, once the results were official, Madison got busy reorganizing his Cabinet, finally replacing his incompetent secretaries of war and the navy.

THE WAR OF 1813

By 1813 Madison's grandiose plan to bring England quickly to its knees had failed. With the exception of New England, the eastern

Commodore Oliver Perry is rowed to the Niagara *where the British squadron was defeted.*

seaboard was patrolled by a British blockade. English forces routinely raided American villages. Looking to win a victory on land, the new secretary of war, John Armstrong, pointed American troops once again toward Canada. On April 27 the American army finally enjoyed some success, taking the town of York (present-day Toronto). Not only did American troops capture the city, they burned the Parliament building to the ground—an act that came back to haunt them when the British took Washington a year later. In May American troops also captured Fort George, forcing the British withdrawal from Lake Erie. Unfortunately, these victories were followed by a blunder.

Two American generals, John Chandler and William Winder, became separated from their troops and were captured in the Battle of Stony Creek. With that catastrophe, the second attempt to take Canada failed.

President Madison was not happy. That summer he was so ill that Dolley feared he would not recover. She wrote, "It has been three weeks since I have nursed him night and day. Sometimes I despair!" Eventually Madison was well enough to travel to Montpelier for a vacation. There he received good news. Navy Commodore Oliver Hazard Perry had defeated the British and taken control of Lake Erie. Perry famously wrote to his commanders stationed on land, "We have met the enemy and they are ours." In October General William Henry Harrison, later America's ninth president, defeated British and Native American forces at the Battle of the Thames.

WASHINGTON BURNS

Despite some American victories, the United States could not win the war. Indeed, although the performance of the American navy had far exceeded anyone's expectations, it was ultimately outgunned by the British. In April of 1814 Napoleon was defeated in Russia, allowing British troops to concentrate more seriously on their assault on America. Having assembled ten thousand troops, the British prepared to march into New York, first bringing in supplies over Lake Champlain. Only a dramatic naval victory on September 11, 1814, led by Commander Thomas Macdonough, was able to force a British retreat.

At the same time, however, a second British force of some four thousand men had landed in the Cheaspeake Bay area of Maryland. In August British troops marched 35 miles overland,

Upon strict British orders, Washington, D.C.'s, government buildings were burned in the War of 1812.

easily dispersing American militiamen, and were soon at the out-skirts of Washington. As British troops approached the capital, many in Washington worried that Madison would flee. Instead, he showed great courage, riding on horseback to meet troops and direct military operations. As British troops entered Washington, Madison returned to the White House to help his wife get away. Dolley dashed off a quick letter to her sister, saying, "I must leave this house, or the retreating army will make me a prisoner in it by filling up the road I am directed to take. . . . [W]here I shall be tomorrow, I cannot tell!"

Soon British Commander George Cockburn was in the White House. There he poured a glass of Madison's wine and proposed a toast to "Jemmy's health." After that, as payback for what the American army had done at York (Toronto), the British forces set fire to much of the city before withdrawing. As Washington was burning, Madison checked on troop movements and went back to the capital. Knowing that it would boost the country's morale to see the government in action, Madison kept his cool—by that point he had been on horseback almost constantly for nearly four days and nights—and called Congress back for a session. A wealthy Virginian offered his home to Madison, and he and Dolley moved into the Octagon House, which became a temporary Executive Mansion.

With Madison back in the seat of power, the war eventually moved north to Baltimore. There, Americans held off British attacks at Fort McHenry in a battle that inspired Francis Scott Key to pen the words that would become the national anthem.

THE WAR ENDS

In late 1812 Madison got a welcome surprise. At that point Napoleon was invading Russia, and Czar Alexander I did not want his country's British ally to waste firepower in North America. To free Britain to concentrate her armies in Europe and Asia, the czar offered to mediate the disagreements between the United States and England. In response, Madison sent a team of Americans, including war hawk Henry Clay and future president John Quincy Adams, to negotiate a peace in the city of Ghent, now part of Belgium. At first American failures on the battlefield gave Britain the upper hand in the negotiations. England demanded control of the Great Lakes and part of Maine. They also wanted a Native-American buffer zone between the

United States and Canada. But in late 1814, when news of American victories in New York and Baltimore reached overseas, Britain was suddenly put on the defensive. Exhausted from years of battle with Napoleon, the British realized that they did not have the energy to take a serious fight to the American shores. By that time Madison was so eager to end the fighting that he was willing to sign an agreement that did not even call for Britain to stop impressing American sailors. In the end it was easier to declare a truce and go home.

The Treaty of Ghent was signed on Christmas Eve in 1814. Both sides agreed to stop fighting. Conquered territory was given back. No mention was made of the Orders of Council or the Native-American menace in the West. Though the treaty failed to mention impressment, over time the British stopped the practice anyway. With the Napoleonic Wars over, the British navy reverted to a peacetime footing, and its need for sailors diminished.

Sadly, even after the treaty was signed, the fighting did not stop—at least not yet. As word of the treaty slowly made its way back to the United States, American troops achieved a stirring victory over the British in New Orleans. Ironically, the battle that made its general, Andrew Jackson, a national hero and later propelled him to the presidency never needed to be fought.

MADISON'S LONG GOOD-BYE

*D*uring the war, Madison was hated by many of his countrymen. But when the terms of the Treaty of Ghent were made public, the country celebrated. Madison told Congress, "The late war, although reluctantly declared by Congress, had become a necessary resort to assert the rights and independence of the nation."

Looking back, it's hard to disagree with him—even though the War of 1812 achieved none of America's stated war claims. Britain didn't give up an inch of territory or the right to impress U.S. sailors. But by standing up to the British, America had shown the world that it was a country to be reckoned with—a nation that would fight for its rights. A French minister, Louis Serurier, wrote, "[T]he war has given the Americans what they so essentially lacked, a national character." In 1815 the Federalist president John Adams wrote a friend:

> *Mr. Madison's administration has proved great points, long disputed in Europe and America.*
>
> *1. He has proved that an administration, under our present Constitution, can declare war.*
> *2. That it can make peace.*
> *3. That, money or no money, government or no government, Great Britain can never conquer this country or any considerable part of it.*

The Federalization of the Jeffersonians

Ironically, while the Republican Party became the dominant political party in the years following the War of 1812, it did so by embracing Federalist policies. Thomas Jefferson had envisioned a country of farmers in which the rights of the individual states ruled supreme. Instead, under his own presidency and that of James Madison, the governing of the United States became centered more on what was happening in Washington. The historian Garry Wills wrote:

> *Jefferson had opposed the Bank of the United States, public debt, a navy, a standing army, American manufacturing, federal[ly] funded improvement of the interior, the role of a world power, military glory, an extensive foreign ministry, loose construction of the Constitution, and the subordination of the states to the federal government.*

To wage war against England, James Madison had to recharter the bank, build up the armed forces, put American manufacturing to work on behalf of the war effort, get actively involved in foreign affairs, and wield federal supremacy over the states. It is understandable then that John Randolph complained that the Republicans won by losing their souls.

Adams went on to compliment America's generals and its navy. Interestingly, his list of Madison's achievements are all things modern Americans would take for granted. But in 1812 the United States was still proving itself as a nation. For a young country still finding its footing in the world, Mr. Madison's War was, indeed, America's second revolution.

The War of 1812 did something else, too: it finally turned James Madison into a popular president. When the Treaty of Ghent reached American shores, a nationalist fervor swept across the country. All wrongs were forgiven. The fighting men of the navy and army were honored heroes. Madison was heralded as a wise leader. Dolley gave so many parties that their new quarters became known as "the house with a thousand candles." With the country finally at peace, Madison was able to put his mind to domestic issues. He proposed that Congress provide money to build roads and canals and to establish a national university. With victory on the battlefield, the Democratic-Republicans became the dominant political party in the country. In 1816 James Monroe, who had served as Madison's secretary of war and state, was easily elected as America's fifth president, leaving the old Federalist Party all but defunct.

Back to Montpelier

At the end of Madison's presidency in 1817, Dolley Madison wanted desperately to travel to Paris. But James Madison wanted nothing more than to spend the rest of his life at Montpelier—which is exactly what he did, running his plantation, reading books, and writing letters.

Over time Madison took pride in how his country was growing and how well his Constitution was holding up. When Thomas

After his second term as president ended, James Madison returned to his childhood home of Montpelier in Virginia.

Jefferson and John Adams both died on July 4, 1826, Madison was surprised to realize that he was the last founding father alive. He wrote, "Having outlived so many of my contemporaries, I ought not to forget that I may be thought to have outlived myself." But in 1829, at age seventy-eight, Madison was lured back to politics a final time, serving as a delegate to a convention set up to revise Virginia's constitution. Later, in his eighties, Madison was saddened to discover that the ideas of the Kentucky and Virginia resolutions he wrote in 1798 with Thomas Jefferson were being co-opted by proslavery southerners looking for legal justification to secede from the Union. Indeed, Madison's feelings toward slavery caused him great pain in his later years. Until the end he thought the practice detestable. Even so, he could not figure out a way the southern economy could survive without such free labor, and he owned slaves his entire life.

In the end Madison outlived Thomas Jefferson and John Adams by ten years, dying on June 28, 1836, at Montpelier at the age of eighty-five. He was buried at his family plantation. His tombstone was the shape of an obelisk and, along with the dates of his birth and death, bore only one word: Madison. After his death Dolley eventually had to sell Montpelier to pay off debts run up by her son, Payne. She then moved back to Washington, where she was welcomed again into society life with open arms. She died at age eighty-one. Though first buried in Washington, ten years after her death friends raised the money to move her remains back to Montpelier.

THE MADISON LEGACY

Throughout his life James Madison always looked up to his older friend Thomas Jefferson. But "the great little Madison" might well

Madison wrote James Monroe in 1831, "In explanation of my microscopic writing, I must remark that the older I grow my stiffening fingers make smaller letters, as my feet take smaller steps."

be Jefferson's historical equal. Like any leader, he had his flaws. A better thinker than natural leader, he bungled the first part of the War of 1812. Like most politicians, his positions on issues of the day weren't always consistent throughout his career. But Madison's gifts to the country far outweigh any negatives. Without his efforts, our Constitution and Bill of Rights might well have never been written. Once the Constitution was the law of the land, no one fought harder to uphold its values. Many wartime presidents have used war as an excuse to expand their executive powers. But Madison was always careful to act in accordance with the Constitution he helped to create. In the end the main act of his presidency, the War of 1812, turned out to be a success. Other presidents might have continued to dodge the fight with England or even have gone to war with France. Under James Madison's leadership, the United States grew up. By battling the British to a draw, the United States proved that it was ready to join other nations as an equal partner on the world stage.

A driving force in the formation of the Constitution and one of the nation's founding fathers, James Madison left this advice to his country: "The advice nearest to my heart and deepest in my convictions, that the Union of the states be cherished and perpetuated."

1751
Born in Port Conway, Virginia

1771
Graduates from the College of New Jersey (now Princeton University)

1776
Serves as a delegate to the Virginia Constitutional Convention; argues for freedom of religion

1777
Appointed to the Virginia Council of State

1780
Becomes a delegate to the Continental Congress

1789
Elected to the House of Representatives and leads the effort to enact the Bill of Rights

1794
Marries widow Dolley Payne Todd

1797
Leaves government to return to Montpelier

1750

1798
Joins with Thomas Jefferson to write the Virginia and Kentucky resolutions

1799
Elected to the Virginia state legislature

1801
Appointed America's secretary of state

1809
Becomes America's fourth president

1817
Retires to Montpelier

1829
Serves as a delegate to a Virginia constitutional convention

1836
Dies on June 28 at age eighty-five

1840

GLOSSARY

anarchy state of lawlessness due to absence of government

blockade the closing off, as a port, harbor, or city, by hostile ships or troops to prevent entrance or exit

boycott to refuse to have dealings with a person, store, or country to express disapproval over a policy

caucus a closed meeting of people belonging to the same political party

commission to appoint to a position or rank in the armed forces

delegates people who are designated to act for or represent others

depose remove from power

embargo an order of government prohibiting movement of merchant ships into or out of certain ports

encroachment entering by gradual steps or by stealth into the possessions or rights of another

Federalists supporters of the Federalist Party, supporting a strong central government

fiscal pertaining to money and its management

independent standing alone

liberal favorable to progress or reform

majority the number greater than half the total

mercenaries hired soldiers

minority the number less than half the total

nullification the voiding or cancelling of a law

orator a public speaker, usually of great note

ratify to confirm by expressing consent, approval, or formal sanction

FURTHER INFORMATION

BOOKS

January, Brendan. *James Madison: America's 4th President*. Danbury, CT: Children's Press, 2003.

Kozleski, Lisa. *James Madison* (Childhoods of the Presidents). Broomall, PA: Mason Crest Publishers, 2002.

Mitchell, Barbara. *Father of the Constitution: A Story about James Madison*. Minneapolis: Lerner Publishing Group, 2004.

Santella, Andrew. *James Madison* (Profiles of the Presidents). New York: Compass Point Books, 2002.

WEB SITES

The White House

http://www.whitehouse.gov/history/presidents/jm4.html

At the official Web site of the White House, explore a brief presidential biography of James Madison, as well as links to those of other presidents.

The James Madison Center

http://www.jmu.edu/madison/center/main_pages/madison_archives/quotes/ownwords.htm

This Web site offers a compilation of quotations from the letters of James Madison.

Founding Fathers

http://www.foundingfathers.info/

This Web site explores the early history of the nation, with information on *The Federalist Papers*, the American flag, U.S. historical portraits of the nation's founding fathers, and notable quotations.

BIBLIOGRAPHY

Adams, Henry. *The United States in 1800*. New York: Charles Scribner's Sons, 1889.

Bailey, Thomas A. *The American Pageant: A History of the Republic*, Vols. 1 & 2, Fifth Edition. Lexington, MA: D. C. Heath and Company, 1975.

Collier, Christopher, and James Lincoln Collier. *Decision in Philadelphia: The Constitutional Convention of 1787*. New York: Ballantine Books, 1986.

Davis, Kenneth C. *Don't Know Much About History*. New York: Avon Books, 1990.

Ellis, Joseph J. *Founding Brothers: The Revolutionary Generation*. New York: Alfred A. Knopf, 2000.

Hofstadter, Richard. *Great Issues in American History: From the Revolution to the Civil War, 1765–1865*. New York: Vintage Books, 1958.

Polikoff, Barbara Garland. *James Madison*. Ada, OK: Garrett Educational Corporation, 1989.

Rutland, Robert Allan. *James Madison: The Founding Father*. Columbia and London: University of Missouri Press, 1987.

Wills, Garry. *James Madison* (The American Presidents Series). New York: Henry Holt, 2002.

INDEX

Pages in **boldface** are illustrations.

★ ★ ★ ★ ★ ★ ★ ★ ★ ★ ★ ★ ★ ★ ★ ★ ★ ★ ★ ★

ABOUT THE AUTHOR

Dan Elish is the author of numerous history books for children, including *Theodore Roosevelt*, *The Trail of Tears*, and *Vermont* for Benchmark Books. He has also written several novels for young readers. He lives in New York City with his wife and two children.